CHANGING ROADS

MOTORCYCLE POETRY AND MORE

CHANGING ROADS

MOTORCYCLE POETRY AND MORE

TF SNEIDER

authorHOUSE®

AuthorHouse™ LLC
1663 Liberty Drive
Bloomington, IN 47403
www.authorhouse.com
Phone: 1-800-839-8640

Published by AuthorHouse 05/14/2014

ISBN: 978-1-4969-1064-6 (sc)
ISBN: 978-1-4969-1065-3 (e)

Contents

INTRODUCTION

I asked myself some questions of late, "What makes us so deeply interested in those hobbies, games, or passions we become deeply involved with, and why do we pursue them?" I imagine to everyone their interests differ, such as golf, hunting, painting, and like myself—poetry. Something, or someone must make the interest "grow", plant a trial seed, another 'someone' knowingly or unknowingly fertilized it, and yet another added a little water or sunlight. Do we play golf on our own without ever seeing the game? Go hunting without being shown or not knowing why we ever purchase a license to do so? Attempt painting, not knowing which colors or medium on which to leave our mark?

We owe the majority of our education to our parents, mostly by observance than by any "book" education. But, my Mother or Father never golfed or hunted, yet I do them whenever the season comes and its convenient. They would never own a motorcycle, yet I own two at present, and I enjoy them passionately. I did however, pick up on poetry, a hobby of my mother's in her teenage years. She wrote passionately up to her marriage, then her writing tapered off with nothing documented after she was about 40 years of age. In her teenage notes for example:

TO CHESTER

By Marie E. Mackley

I wrote a letter
Sealed it, too . . .
Licked the stamp
It was for you
But I just couldn't
I wouldn't Mail it.
For in it's
A message saying,
"We're through!"
It can't be over
I like you still
But if I don't mail it,
Mother will!

One of the last poems Mother wrote, that I
know of, and had published was this.

PRIVATE CONVERSATION

By Marie E. Sneider
"TRIBUTE TO TRIUMPH" Exposition Press 1947

God looked down from His throne and smiled
I'm sure, when He heard him say,
"I think we'll go out underneath the tree
And talk to God today.
Suppose He knows the fun we've had,
The spankin's too, for being bad,
The scolding I got for looking grim
When Daddy asked a favor for him?
Funny, when I squashed that bug
I'm sure sorry he's all dead
And that worm sure weren' goin' no where
When I quick snapped off his head.
D'ya suppose He's going to listen
When I tell Him the fun I had,
Guess it wasn't me to blame . . .
Twas the <u>imp</u> in me who was bad!"

My mother had 4 sons and I believe my Mother was talking about my 2 oldest brothers, as two of us weren't born when this was written.

I am the opposite as I didn't pick up on poetry with any zeal till after I approached 40. I hated high school English class yet along my life's road my mother, a few of my teachers, especially my ninth grade English teacher Mrs. Skulas, and a couple others, read to us or had us read various poems. Some of them stuck and stuck hard, such as Robert Service's "The Cremation of Sam McGee", Joyce Kilmer's "Trees", and Alfred Lord Tennyson's "Crossing of the Bar" to name a few. Later in life, as I was raising kids, my wife and I would read to them out of children's books by Shel Silverstein, and I would sing to them memorized folk tunes. Interestingly, I found in some of my

Father's Playboy Magazines adult poems written by Shel Silverstein such as "The Yellow Haired Woman" and "Plastic, Only Plastic", and like in high school, they stuck like glue. Mr. Silverstein made a big impression on me, and upon his death in May of 1999, I emailed this to a colleague, Merri Flisnik,

I ONLY KNEW HIS PEN

How the heart aches from the loss of this sensitive man. One who pours his soul's blood across paper through his pen. A mind that flies a trapeze above the net-less earth of life, spinning, twisting, somersaults with joy, and touching the deepest inner most self.

So that others may cry, reflect, and laugh.

Thanks Shel!"

So it started with me back in the 1980s, while waiting for my Chapter of Ohio Eastern Stars to formally perform their 20 minute opening ceremony, I would jot down a couple lines and recite them in the same meeting.

When I was inspired, which wasn't very often, I would write some lines and would tuck them away not knowing what I was saving them for. I was asked to write poems for my friend's special occasions, so being challenged I would. Some lines rattled around in my head with such ferocity that I would stay up most of a night trying to meter it on paper, and yet, others spilled in just minutes on the keyboard like water from a spigot. Many were recited on stage at the famous Caffe Lena, on Philo Street in Saratoga Springs, America's oldest folk music coffee house, where you will find me on the first Wednesday of every month. You will find the majority of my poetry here, a collection of life's happenings and inspirations. I hope you enjoy them as much as I enjoyed writing and reciting them.

Dedicated to:

Marie E. Sneider

So your energy lives on.

CHANGING ROADS

We take roads for travel.
We take roads for granted.
We take roads to unravel
Life's songs previously chanted.

The same roads we take to work.
The same roads we take to play.
Only change their overcoat
And take you a "familiar" way.

But, hundreds of years of Indian trail
Change by different rolling wheels
Miles of sand and gravel path
Change to concrete and steel.

How do we re-visit a region
Of our life in the earlier day?
By riding back thru roads to legions
Of former haunts, friends, and play.

Ah, the roads of my former life
And the crossroads of other souls
Change by the ravage of time
Change all our values and goals

As I ride down Six Mile Road
Out of Sault Ste Marie
Past the gambling casinos, the Cozy Inn,
And to the town of Brimley.

Past the Bay Mills Indian Homes
Of the famous Chippewa Tribe.
Along the shores of Whitefish bay
On Two-wheeled steel I ride.

I took a left up West Tower Road
40 years ago mentally I slide
To a steep cliff over Spectacle Lake,
An Indian Cemetery on the other side.

How just 40 years has changed this place
From a peaceful, tranquil view.
To resort houses, playgrounds, and parks
For the rich and privileged few.

And just on the other side of the road
The Mission Hill Indian Cemetery lay
Centuries of serene resting souls
Disturbed constantly by the "modern day".

Ah, the roads of my former life
And the crossroads of other souls
Change by the ravage of time
Change by our values and goals.

I rolled down the wooded lane
Under canopies of maples and oaks.
To the corner of Dollar Settlement
And memories of its elderly folks.

There used to be a hamburger stand
And a friendly variety store,
Just past the small white Christian church
None are there, anymore.

Just down the road was Pendles Swamp
Lois and Agnes DeMerse lived there
In a two-room log Cabin
With the partridge, beaver, and bear.

I used to stay with friend, Dick Splan
On the corner of South Plantation Road.
Where we hunted and fished the area land
My God, how the memories unfold!

Lakeshore Drive to Bay View Park,
To set camp and rest for the day.
And peacefully sleep on Lake Superior's shores
To the rolling waters of Whitefish Bay.

Ah, the roads of my former life
And the crossroads of other souls
Change by the ravage of time
Change by our values and goals.

A cool brisk morning and fresh lake air
I pack up my scoot and head west.
Along Gitche Gumee's Lakeshore drive
And an unknown, never-ending quest.

40 years ago this flat pavement was gravel
Passed the Naomagong and Pendles streaming
Where the speckled trout danced on our lines
With the Smelt and Rainbow teaming.

Abe Lablah, the Chippewa Chief,
Wet a line with Dick and I.
Now neither walk the trickling shore.
From my eye, a tear; my breath, a sigh.

I've lost the smell of the cedar and pine.
I've lost the sound of crashing waves.
I enter a maze of houses and roads
And I seem to lose my way.

The shoreline has changed to public beaches
The woods changed to residential squat.
Roads, please take me from this place
What once seemed Utopian, now, is **NOT**!

Ah, the roads of my former life
And the crossroads of other souls
Change by the ravage of time
Change by our values and goals.

We take roads for travel.
We take roads for granted.
We take roads to unravel
Life's songs previously chanted.

NOTE: This poem has unique character. It is written in 14 line Sonnet form. The odd numbered lines rhyme internally, and the even numbered lines all rhyme to the title. That makes 21 lines all rhyme to the word "line", three of which are the title and the other 18 do not repeat any rhymed words.

THREE FEET RIGHT OF THE LINE

I'm tired of the strife in everyday life,
And **former** friends once benign.
And I don't give a squat if the boss gets too hot
Or that production is in decline.
My ambition is sagging and the ol' lady's been nagging;
She's trying to give me a sign.
The kids have all grown, and from the nest they have flown
To other towns they made a beeline.
With roof leaks on the shed, all the flowers are dead
And I lost my faithful canine.
I'll just pack up my gear and get the **HELL out of here**
Before my soul dies **black** on the vine.
Taking the 2-wheeled mode, I'll FLY down the road
Riding . . . **three feet right of the line.**

With a smile and a sigh I'll wave them goodbye,
And bid them "Auld Lang Syne".
The road has its woes, and pickins' for the crows,
And hazards come rain or come shine.
Like the center of the road is no place to behold
So greasy it will leave you supine.
In the far right lane you could end up in pain
By bigger vehicles you're hidden behind.
The Cager's phone chat can leave you dead flat,
Or with the tar-crack road serpentine.
But, with the wind in my hair, **I can handle that fare**
Feeling relaxed and simply divine.
So I'll roll away the miles with bugs in my smile,
Riding . . . **three feet right of the line.**

I won't have a hitch with my God 'ridin-bitch'
And a nose-hit of cedar and pine.
Thru the mountains we'll climb, wasting my time,
At peace and completely sublime.
At night I will sleep, without counting sheep,
Where stars and fire-flys entwine.
In the morning we'll rise, get the sleep from my eyes,
Load the scoot in the early sunshine.
Within my battered soul, We'll mend that gapping hole
And suckle on life's sweetened wine.
Then We'll return to the start with a much lighter heart
With my friends I'll gladly consign.
Feeling unhindered and free on my two-wheeled RV
Riding . . .

. . . <u>Three Feet Right of the Line.</u>

TRANQUILITY

I laid upon her firm foundation within her warm flannel nest.
My back was supported against the headboard by a stack of feather pillows.
She lay between my out stretched legs, her tresses drape my chest.
Our passions have been sated and our limbs heavy as the willow's.

The fragrance of our love mingled with the Jasmine in her hair.
So warm, so soft, so tender is her formerly sweat dampened skin.
A full winter moon illuminates the snow laden lawn where,
Its radiance is the only light causing night's slumber to begin.

WINDOW GAZING

My soul is anchored 'tween heaven and hell,
Dodging and ducking verbal abuse as I must.
I cannot escape this nightmare-like shell,
What evil arrow does *his* wicked bow thrust?

Winter is upon my house and my heart.
Pacing the floor till my heal spurs ache.
Through mental windows I seek a new part
To the values of **life**, now at stake.

Through these frosted windows I see passion and joy
For this painfully empty, bruised and battered soul.
Must I be treated as trinket or toy?
Is legal relief my only goal?

What evil stirs in the menaced mind,
Of powers that can **squelch** this torment I bare.
Dark, devious thoughts, of various kind,
Release me through to my frosted stare.

Note: *The word "his" can be exchanged with the word "her" for the reader's satisfaction.*

BITTER AND SWEET

This time of the year we wish for sun.
We wish for green grass in which to run.
We shun the rain and especially the snow.
We cannot wait for the sunshine to glow. But . . .
I am one who likes the rain and especially the snow.
I like to see it come, and I like to see it go.
Without these we'd have no trees and have no grass
We'd be without shade and can't bare our—feet.
This summer midst two months of heat and drought,
When the ball games are canceled and the water runs out,
When the sweat runs down the middle of your back,
You'll pray for those white fluffy clouds to turn black.
So tonight when we get that rain, snow, or sleet.
Stop and contemplate, which is bitter and which is sweet.

In "Down at Sully's East", the location is real, but the people and actual happenings are fictitious. The proprietor, Bella Harrington, gave me permission to use her name and the name of her establishment, located at Prospect and Maple in Glens Falls, NY. My hangout, Sully's East, is the oldest Irish tavern in Glens Falls approaching 100 years of age.

DOWN AT SULLY'S EAST

While cruising Glens Falls, my thirstiness calls
As I'm tired of shiftin' thru gears.
"I'll stop, what the heck, down on Prospect
At Sully's East for a tall glass of beer."

This lonely old coot, crawled off of his scoot
And entered in Sully's front door.
I weren't very able to find a small table
My back was tired and butt quite sore.

Well don't ya know, 'Suicide Shift' Joe
Was tending to the patrons that day.
I waved to the keep, "Bring me somethin' that's cheap.
How much am I expected to pay?"

At a corner table sat 'Crazy Bitch Mabel'
And her dude, skinny Mick McGee.
Mick seemed well dressed, maybe wearin' his best
Something of a sight to see.

"Beer!" shouted Mick; he gave a fifty a flick
And it landed near Mabel's derriere.
Mick said, "Old Nag Mabel get your ass off my table.
That fifty is for the beer."

Out came Joe with Mick's picture of woe
And a shot of Jack for his dear Mabel.
She tossed it straight down, with a wince and a frown,
Then slammed the glass down hard on the table.

"Mick I'm tired of you, you don't wanna screw,
You only drink gallons of beer.
I've had enough, Don't like it; TOUGH!!
I'll hook with that biker over there."

I looked all around; looked up, looked down
But I was the only biker I could see.
She staggered on over to this dusty old rover,
I said, "Ma'am, You talking about me?"

"Now I don't care if you ruff up me hair
Or rub your tits from my ear to my ear.
But Mabel, **Sweet** Mabel, keep your ass off my table
My three dollars is for the beer".

Well . . ., my poor rapport, which she had once before,
Just got her really quite pissed.
So her fist she let fly aiming straight at my eye,
But spun to the floor because she missed.

So the whole bar's riff-raff broke out in a laugh
And a calamity started to commence.
I began to wobble hit by a chair and a bottle,
Mick . . . he was gone and over the fence.

"Adios Joe, I gotta go!"
While three patrons gave me the boot.
Out in the street sitting high on my seat
Was Mabel astride of my scoot.

"What in the hell are you doing Gal?
Do you think your ridin with me?"
She said, "I am sick of that rich prick Mick,
And now I'm a-skatin' out free.

I had a strange itch to like this little witch,
If she wants this dirty old coot.
Cause this ain't no fable, for my dear sweet Mabel
Is riding bitch on the back of me scoot.

SULLY'S EAST—REVISITED

(Sigh) It's the first of December and its easy to remember
The miles and the sun on our face.
Riding through the hill and the twisting thrills
As memories pour from the warm fireplace.

Mabel said "Oh Dear Lord, let's grab the ol' Ford.
And get the hell out of here."
"Where would we go in this damn cold snow."
I said with a frown and a sneer.

"I know a place that'll put a smile on your face
You may even shed a tear."
Said Mabel, "At least, Lets raid Sully's East
And have a tankard of beer."

"Let's Go Tramp, turn off the lamp,
And we'll get us a corner table.
I have no doubt; Bella won't throw us out,
After all, you're hangin' with Mabel."

We entered the door I was thrown through before
And greeted Bella with a smile.
She got in my face, said, "Behave in my place,
Or in jail you'll sit for a while."

"The last time here, a drinkin' your beer
You tore up most of my place."
I said, "Yes Mame, I'll act like a lamb."
And screwed a smile, wide on my face.

The barmaid was Sue, and she hadn't a clue
Of what went on that hot summer day.
Without any fear she brought us some beer
And for the same amount of pay.

"Hey Bella, What happened to Mick, that skinny little prick?
Does he show his face anymore?"
She said, "Not since you and Mable broke half of my tables
And tore the hinges clean off the door."

That door flew open wide and a mountain came inside
By the name of Big Dan Fagan.
The whole place shuttered as he stumbled and stuttered
Like he just fell off the wagon.

Dan said,
"Hey barmaid there, with the long curly hair,
Give me a double of Tullamore Dew.
Hell, fill up the glass, my little Irish lass."
And he tossed it down PDQ.

Bella said with a grin, "I am not tryin' to sin,
But that's twenty bucks for a glass that size.
So cough up the dough or out you will go".
And she looked him square in the eyes.

Dan grabbed her wrist and gave it a twist
And it brought Mabel straight to attention.
Then so it began, kickin' the ass of Big Dan
OH! and I forgot to mention.

That it took a few more to throw his butt out the door
Just few more tables and chairs
A few bars of soap, and 30 feet of rope
And a few cuts from broken stoneware.

A hot pot of beef stew, and a cue stick or two
Mabel inserted in places unknown.
Through the door, 'Ker-plop', in the arms of a cop
We three landed with a moan and a groan.

"Throw their asses in jail, and give them no bail."
Yelled Bella from the door of the bar.
Covered in mud, and a little of Dan's blood
The cop stuffed us in the back his car.

Down the road we flew, blowing the siren too
As if we committed a crime.
Mable said with a smile, you could see for a mile
"You sure know how to have a good time".

THE ACCIDENT

I was asked
    on the gurney
If I was
    still gon'na ride.

My response
    was too simple,
"I'll ride on,
    even if I die."

RIDING AUTUMN

Oh heavy autumn air,
How you make my ride that much sweeter.
Passing your majestic fragrant foliage;
Dazzling the eyes of this witness.
Your stay is short; my yearning long.

Far I ride, twisting, turning,
Color-splashed mountain roads,
And ponder the deepened music of the iron horse.
Stay music . . . Stay awhile . . .,
As I fear the upcoming snows.

LIFE'S COUNTRY GARDEN

We all have fond memories of life's country garden, and it's different for each of mankind.

Whether you're rich or poor, city or country, it's all according to your state of mind.

The youngest of four boys, who raised chickens and ducks, on a small two acre farm.

In a depression built house, one bath and root cellar, and a space heater to keep us warm.

We had an antique tractor to till the ground, with steel wheels and triangular spikes.

Piloted by Dad, a diligent brick mason, raising crops for his hungry four tykes.

Have you ever planted corn with a hand held corn planter, or had kittens born in your bed?

Plucked apples from a tree, or used kerosene to get jiggers from the hair on your head?

The clothes that I had were kinda tattered and worn, for they had fit three other backs.

We had new shirts, lovingly at Christmas, sewn by Mom from chicken feed sacks.

We all have fond memories of life's country garden, and it's different for each of mankind.

Whether you're rich or poor, city or country, it's all according to your state of mind.

You see, deep in life's soil that old antique tractor, cut a furrow of riches galore,

Not of gold or of silver, but things very precious, like tolerance, adaptability, and more.

Like kindness and charity, sharing with others, and house paint for daddy's old car.

Like swimmin' in a creek, the value of hugs, and work at the church's bazaar.

Have you ever hunted bunnies with an old farm dog and a forked maple slingshot?

Or the collection of pennies, and Indian nickels, not knowing the wealth that you've got.

Was it delivering papers for a few extra bucks, or mowing lawn for the widow next door?

Counting the days till the chicken's eggs hatch, or shooting rats on the pigeon coop floor.

We all have fond memories of life's country garden, and it's different for each of mankind.

Whether you're rich or poor, city or country, it's all according to your state of mind.

Like plucking a chicken, hoeing the beans, or cleaning a bucket of perch. Food baskets for the poor, cancer pads for old veterans, serving Mass at St. Clement's church.

Ya know all the memories come pouring back home when I hear every now and then

A great old tune by a non-famous singer by the name of Walter Brennan.

"One of these days I'm gonna climb that mountain, walk up there among them clouds,

Where the cotton's high and the corn's a growin' and there ain't no fields to plow."

I have fond memories of life's country garden where things seem simple and free.

As I gaze across golden fields I dream of an old tractor, my father, and me.

The above picture is a restored 1938 Sears Roebuck & Co. "Handiman". It is owned at the time of this writing by Jim Opersal of Blissfield, MI. The one owned by my Father was identical, but not nearly as good looking, as our's was rusty and mud covered from years of hard work. My Father's Handiman had many attachments such as a single plow, disc cultivator, and a sickle bar we used for cutting down weeds along our creek. There was a hay rake that could be pulled behind, but I had never seen it attached as we never cut / bailed hay. It was powered by a 5 hp Briggs and Straton engine, one speed forward and a reverse.

KING RICHARD'S KNIGHTS

We wake up in the morning and turn on the news.
Why listen to this crap, we'd much rather snooze.
We hear the screams and we hear the pleas,
We hear words exploited by political parties.
We hear terrorist's chant and mindless shout
Twisting their religion inside out.
"Infidel", "Blasphemer", "Heretic", "Scum" . . .
From where on earth do these bastards come?
They torture, rape, pillage, and kill
Does this sick power give them a thrill?
Many centuries ago when the evil grew
An Old Head of State knew what to do.
He called on great fighters from sea to sea,
And created the forces of King Richard's Army.

I know a large group of Patriots today.
Who don't mind defending this U. S. of A.
Most are battle tried, and scarred by years
Most love to kick ass and show no fear.
They'll protect their families, neighbors, and friends
You can 'bet yer ass' they will fight to the end.
Their leathers are chainmail, their bandana a mask.
Their horse; roaring steel for freedom's task.
Riding Victorys, Indians, and Harleys by name
Rice Burners, will work, but not quite the same.
They'll come from Tampa, even from Houston,
Gather from all cities in America's Union.
A mighty force built from sea to sea
And call themselves, "King Richard's Army".

A Biker may smoke, toke, or toss booze.
But against terrorism they WILL NOT loose.
Engrained in their mind are the former strikes,
Beheadings of innocents, and other dislikes,
Remember our embassies, the Cole, 9-11?
They'll send them bastards anywhere but heaven.
Won't make a difference if you're Muslim or Jew,
Christian, or Hindu here's a warning for you.
If they receive word you are terrorist shit
They'll scoot on over to pay a visit.
And you'll hear the thunder and feel the roar,
A warning sign you cannot ignore,
Your days are numbered and they accept no plea
And deliver the wrath from "King Richard's Army".

Oh, what a nice thought! Oh, what a nice dream!
To end the terrorist's and sick killer's scheme.
To imprison earth's evil, our safeguards release.
To truly live, and ride-on in peace.
Fly to wherever, without baggage check blues.
Take in a movie, without making the news.
To practice our faith, to our deity, pray.
And in our parks watch little kids play.
And strengthen our economy, and create new jobs
To can up some peaches, or grill shish kabob.
Take the 'old Lady' on a road trip or two
To Caribbean water, or Mountain top view
Or ride from the Atlantic to the Pacific sea
Never again needing "King Richard's Army".

PICKINS' FOR THE CROW

Work at 8, on the road by 7.
38 degrees; brisk but clear.
I only have 23 miles to go
Traffic is light; little to fear.

A hundred yards up in the ditch
A bloated dead deer carcass lay.
And perched upon its snout
Was a Crow just pickin' away.

I thought about my ride
And if that deer was me.
And how some too-busy cager
Just didn't happen to see.

If a cager makes a text or calls
When he is supposed to be drivin'
Watches everything but the road
His radio's jumpin' and jivin'.

Do you think for one minute
He's aware to where he goes?
For in one blink of an eye
A biker is pickins' for the crows.

Although bikers party a bit
And tend towards hedonistic
They're very aware of how they ride
Let's be realistic.

Skulls and snakes and long fork rakes
Dark glasses and leather clothes
Display very well we ride towards hell,
And maybe—pickins' for the crows.

Cagers!! Pay attention t'wher your going
Don't just stare at the stripes.
Keep your eyes open, turn down the tunes,
And listen for our pipes.

There's reasons bikers draw attention
Most every where we go.
We don't want to end up
Pickins' for the crow.

WINTER SLEEPING

Its the Autumn's last "Hurrah" outside,
The cold wind churns to curtail my ride.
The cool crisp day is shortened by shrouds
Of the upcoming winter's cold gray clouds.

I curse at the thought of snow and sleet,
And its our last ride along Main Street.
We'll turn in the drive and open the garage
To park by the truck and can of garbage.

Remove my brain bucket, and uncovered my hands,
Lean back and admire the way she stands.
I give her a pat and smile rather forlorn
Remembering spring when we were reborn.

Reflecting on adventures in the summer sun,
From Boston's coast to Lake Michigan,
From the Thousand Islands to the Penn State hills,
For hundreds of miles of twisting thrills.

You have flown uncomplaining carrying my loads,
Soaring endless highways, or down country roads.
I weep 'cause the summer has come to an end.
You're a faithful companion and a well trusted friend.

Tomorrow I'll give you a bath, then park you deep
In the garage, where you will quietly sleep.
When you awake under spring's warm sky.
I'll fire you up
and away
WE'LL FLY!

BEER

In the heat of the day working in the garden.
You're knees become sore; you're sweatin' hard n',
You're back is about to lock, along with your gear
It just happens to signal, there ain't enough beer.

With the flowers planted and most of the onions
And you hurt from your nose down to your bunions
And straightening up becomes your greatest fear
It just happens to signal, there ain't enough beer.

When the lawn is cut and so is your will
And your wife claims there more to do still.
Its that kinda crap you don't want to hear.
It just happens to signal, there ain't enough beer.

So trot on down to the local gathering place
And sit around the bar with a smile on your face
You swig on that cold one and grin ear to ear
And you say to the Keep, "there ain't enough beer."

Rollin' Home

I'm on my scoot, dusting off the highway
I'm searching for what made me happy
Down roads I've paved along the way.
Some were very great, some just crappy.

At 19, I joined the military to avoid the draft.
I guess America needed to save the world,
Was it chivalry, or political crap?
I guess my flag wasn't completely unfurled.

I'm rollin', rollin' towards home.

Picked a wonderful girl to become my wife.
Procreation requires responsibility.
They became a major part of my life.
I wonder if it's beyond capability.

Feeling the need to be fiscally sound.
Advance, improve, promote, work HARD!.
Maybe someday I wouldn't be around.
I'll live rich in some graveyard?

Just keep rollin', rollin' home.

34

Kids are grown and their school is done.
Time to live on more than bread and water.
Oops! Who is this? A Grandson?
Followed by more than one granddaughter.

My living become wide, becomes diverse.
I break out from a "Normal" paradigm.
Becoming part of the bigger universe.
All but memories in a very short time.

Downhill rollin', rollin' home.

Time is now the physical issue.
Parts don't heal as they originally did.
Couch potato? Or courageous shrew?
Physically a turd, mentally a kid.

So, a big decision is now at hand
Ride in the wind, or toss an anchor?
On the unknown road I'll take my stand.
Hidden somewhere in life's metaphor.

I'll just keep Rollin', Rollin' home . . .
. . . **Very Soon.**

MY CANDLE

As the years are rolling to an end
And physically I slowly amend,
My life is seen as a melting candle,
In a glass cruet with a small handle.

Once strong and tall and over the rim,
Now a molten mass with light turned dim.
The glass frosted with fading dreams
From living on life's sweetened cream.

The hot pool of wax that remains
Is tarnished with life's endless strain.
Fighting the rain and relentless wind
Of evil thoughts and devilish sin.

I hope that over the burning years
My flame has kindled other spheres
Giving warmth to much finer wax,
Of much softer cotton, or silken flax.

Now, life's fuel slowly runs out
I know for sure, without a doubt,
A dear Friend will cease my feeble roam
And with a gentle hand carry me home.

DREAM . . . MAYBE

Its spring and my butt wants to roam
Pack up the scoot . . . And head out . . .
And head . . . Which way from home?
Down the highway or country route?

Maybe

Mason City Iowa in the west
Or should I say Masonic Grove,
Or it original name Shibboleth.
Thru which the Winnebago Flows.

Where the crackle of gravel roads
Under my wheel's slippery stray
On which Meredith Wilson strode,
And wrote "The Music Man" play.

Where the wind waves fields of wheat
And rustles the corn and beans.
The bread basket of all we eat
By hardened farmers seldom seen.

Maybe . . .

Camping in the Tennessee hills
In Great Smokey National Park.
Where the road twists, winds, n' thrills.
And you become bear bait after dark.

Where steam rises from hillside walls
Where streams gurgle and rivers roar.
Tulip Trees and Oaks stand tall
Where Quail's run and Mockingbirds soar.

Route 129 from Maryville, bring it on,
Riding sober and wide-eyed
Shooting the "Tail of the Dragon"
And Elvis may ask for a ride.
(info: 318 curves in 11 miles of road)

Maybe . . .

To the New England Shore
Riding the paths our country began.
With the Revolutionary War
Breaking away from Great Britain.

The East Coast, Art and History rule.
Writing Poets and Playwright's theme
The home of Ivy League School
Where fishing boats and seafood teem.

Washington DC and Rolling Thunder
On the weekend of Memorial Day.
Raising loud awareness for
Returning POWs and MIAs.

Maybe . . .

Riding the windy plain, or the desert burn,
Does God have a grander scheme?
If only to help me learn,
Within a biker poet's dream.

CAPTAIN OF THE ROAD

Some call Bikers "vagabonds", some "bums",
"One percenters" is easy to believe
Some just think what we do is dumb
I guess that's what most perceive.

Bikers have to work for a livin'
Like most cagers on any given day
Shaking that shitty stick their given.
Setting aside a morsel of pay.

Pay that will get them on the road
Many bikers are migratory
Where they live by a biker's code
And can tell you a rider's story.

Bikers are the uncomfortable class
Not taking a liking to just one spot.
Home is where they park their ass
On a soft seat on an engine that's hot.

Essentials only on the back of their scoots
Just enough till to next stop
A change of cloths, dry pair of boots,
Peanut butter, bread, and some soda pop.

A sleeping bag, tarp, and a bag of tools
Strapped to a sissy or luggage rack
On a custom bike or rugged old school
And maybe a guitar slung oe'r their back.

Sleeping arrangements in different ways.
Seldom with hotels, or a sidewalk wench,
But most seek in a more modest stay
Casting their fart sack on a roadside bench.

Though our pipes cause a ruckus
To alert you when by your side
The attention we draw is a plus
For our efforts to stay alive.

Skulls and snakes on our horse's shell
Dark glasses and leather clothes
Display very well we ride towards hell,
Our final destination, who knows?

Aide and honesty are part of our code
Fear not a leathery, bearded guy
As they rumble down the American road
Sailing off to an endless sky.

Q AND A

Would you ride with me in a driving rain,
When the road turns long and your butt's in pain,
Though rush hour traffic like we're both insane.
Would you ride with me in a driving rain?

Would you ride with me when the road gets rough,
Across rocks, chuck holes, or unpleasant stuff,
When the cushion in your seat just isn't enough,
Would you ride with me when the road gets rough?

Would you ride with me in the chill of night,
When bugs on your glasses blur your sight,
Holding on to me till the morning light,
Would you ride with me in the chill of night?

Would you ride with me on a rusty old bike,
On a cheap military grade look-a-like,
Or asleep on the back of a custom trike,
Would you ride with me on a rusty old bike?

Then I'll ride with you around every bend.
Each moment together we'll gladly transcend,
And gain a new meaning defining "Friend",
Then I'll ride with you around every bend.

Then I will ride with you in the morning sun,
In cloudless skies till the day is done,
When riding alone or a charity run,
Then I'll ride with you and no other one.

Then I'll ride with you over each mountain pass,
Over rolling roads or as flat as glass,
Past fields of corn or prairie grass,
Then I'll ride with you till I breathe my last.

SHADY

Pounding concrete into sand; the interstate rolling under the tread of
my tires;
Seeking "Shady", my ol' lady.

Just yesterday, her disastrous encounter with a truck;
Upon the road, brains explode.

So my Journey began, rolling across the long concrete skin;
A narrow ripple, warm and supple.

As the boarders roll by, the road rises to carry me there;
Winged wheels, roaring steel.

My determined ride divides road's peril yet passionate path;
Sun burns hot, sweating a lot.

The ride soon changes battering me with windy crescendos;
Rain-fresh splash, moistening flesh.

Each State flashes by, along with the time;
My desire flows, emptiness grows.

The concrete path ends to calm the tempest and relax my strength;
A cooling breeze, trembling knees.

Tired and wet, I gratefully stand near the opposing shore;
Demanding friend, journey's end.

I park my ride near Shady's home. Her sweet smell fills my memory;
Her long hair, almost there.

I behold a stark wooden box holds my heaven;
Heart-wrenching grief, NO relief.

With outstretched hands Shady calls with requiem song;
Upon yearning ears, desirous tears.

A Tempestuous Sea
(on our 26th anniversary)

Bouncing champagne corks off the ceiling.
Daytime skinny-dippin' . . . what a feeling.
Broke but happy, losing but winning,
You sure kept my head a-spinning.

Karin and Colleen were added over the years
So were diapers, and heartaches, and tears.
Lodge, n' college, n' family illness kept me gone.
You made dizzy times stable and strong.

Now grandkids and careers make life rather hectic.
No wonder why sights and sounds turn dyslexic.
Being battered and beaten over that tempestuous sea.
Would you sail 26 years more with me?

COLD HUNTING

Morning sun breaks the tops of the hills.
The temperature is well below freezing.
There is dead calm in the air and everything is quiet.
The crunch of footsteps in the snow is not pleasing.

But steps are necessary to reach the hunting stand.
In the stand, I attempt to place myself in some sort of comfort.
Difficult because I can even hear my heart beat and
hair of my ears brushing inside the hood of my sweatshirt.

It is so cold my breath seems to sink, freezing in the air.
Even the brown, stiff leaves that are still on the trees
Flutter back and forth so fast they shutter
With the slightest gust of morning breeze.

The forest is quiet, still, cold, and time passes swiftly.

About a half mile away I can hear the raspy, coarse grackle
Of the raven as it slowly flies toward my hunting garret.
Its lonely calls seek another of its kind, but what for?
For procreation, or another with food in hopes it'll share it?

The sun is up and a squirrel silently bounces along
Seeking one of its latest hidden stash of acorn.
A rabbit bounds a random path to a nearby tree
And parks it butt against its base; quiet, cold, forlorn.

A short burst of wings flutter in nearby trees
And I hear the peep, peep, peep, of a tiny flock of snowbirds.
Shortly after, quickly rushing from tree to tree,
A large Articulated Woodpecker seeks insects, without words.

The forest is quiet, still, and colder, and time passes swiftly.

The light is fading slowly as the sun slips behind the hill
I have seen nothing of the quarry I seek.
He too must be sitting, huddling in some quiet shelter one that allows
him warmth, semi-darkness and a vigilant peek.

Colors fade to hues of browns, grays, and black.
Whatever was green was buried in the blanket of stiffened snow.
My breath has grown ice on my mustache and beard.
My face feels no cold, but my joints move stiff and slow.

The day seemed short, very short, but weirdly interesting.
It's a miracle how the wildlife still live and grow
In this harsh, chilling, barren wintery world.
The night's chill inching down my back tells me to go.

The forest is dark, still, and peaceful as the hunter is gone.

ON DEATH AND DYING

A Henry Van Dyke (1852-1933) Writing modified into Poetry by TFSneider

I'm standing on a wharf near the sea
A large tall ship is moored next to me
She is a thing of beauty; 3 mast and sail
Laden with gold, grain, and bale

The Captain drops her sail and the gentle breeze
Draws the beautiful ship peacefully to sea
We watch her slowly fading goodbye
Till a speck of white 'tween sea and sky

When someone near me said, "She's Gone!"
"Gone where?" Said I with voice quite strong
Is she not as large three mast and sail?
She still has her gold, grain, and bale?

For, I know on some distant shore
Stands 10, 20, or a hundred more,
With bugles blaring and thumping drums
Starts the glad shout, "**There she is! Here she comes!**"

And that is dying.

In Like A Lion

Long shinny jagged leaves with yellow blossoms so fine,
Describes the one and only dreaded dandelion.
I've dug, n'scratched, n'plucked, n'pulled, n' cursed it's roots and spine,
But in the spring my lawn was blessed with that dreaded dandelion.

All summer long I'd *Weed-B-Gone* and *2,4D* it's kind,
But splattered across my barren lawn grew the dreaded dandelion.
Have pleasant thoughts on Father's Day when grandchildren dressed divine,
Bring you hugs and kisses, and a bright bundle of dandelion.

MY COMPANION AND FRIEND

I've done this all before and here I'm doing it again.
Driving to the kennel to get the family a "friend".

That clumsy little black one, looking slightly passive, but alert
I know she'll grow up big, but I guess that won't hurt.
She seems real friendly. She tends to be fun.
She'll make a good companion for my growing son.

What do we name a black ball of hair with white whiskers on her face?
All the names that we bounce around are to common-place.
Big bright eyes, bubbling spirit, and occasionally passes gas.
Only the name of "Pepsi" could give this dog some CLASS!!

She woke at 6 in the morning then played and pranced till dark
Frolicking with my son who taught her how to bark.
The chores my son were given to walk and feed on time
Somehow didn't happen and to quickly became mine.

Pepsi would find her 'dolly' to play toss and tug-a-war
And tired herself to the point in sleep she'd sometimes snore.
At dinner she'd hang around the table, but really didn't beg
She'd stay 'neath the table and maybe rub your leg.

Twice a day Pepsi was fed, and in between, many treats
Like when friends came to visit, that's how they would greet
To encourage her to eat her food, and of course, after for dessert,
And when we came or went, and anytime wouldn't hurt.

Years rolled by, school, sports, and family illness took its toll.
Pepsi was there to cheer me up, she'd calm my burdened soul.
At night when things were quiet, and all were tucked in bed
She'd come and sit by me, on my thigh she'd lay her head.

Early in the morning I'd hear her climb the stair,
To quietly lay beside me, hoping I was unaware
Then when the dawn was breaking, exactly at 6 a.m.,
Your little whine would tell me "Mom, Its time to 'go' again."

How do I cope with the bark and your noisy dialog
You shed enough hair around the house to make another dog.
How many times did you interrupt my favorite TV show?
You'd bark and bark, trot to my coat, "Hey Mom, I gotta GO!!"

Pepsi became my protector, my playmate, and my friend.
A guardian to my household and ever-faithful to the end.
Although Pepsi seemed like trouble, although Pepsi seemed a pain,
I'd trade all of my wealth to be together again.

I bundle you in your blanket, for your years have come to an end.
"Goodbye, My Dearest Companion. Farewell, My Cherished Friend."

No Longing Greater

Pounding gravel into sand; running miles under the tread of my sneakers, I seek the shore,
and more.

Just yesterday, a tempestuous encounter with the past, upon the sea,
a memory.
A labor of passion; rowing a skiff through her siren song, to a distant land,
warm sand.

The Journey began; brushing my oars across her skin, a whispering ripple,
warm and supple.
As the leagues roll by; the sea rises to receive my boat, with thrusting keel,
resisting feel.
The determined skiff; divides her peril and passionate waves, the sun burns hot,
sweating a lot.
Her white caps churn; tossing my craft in crescendos of joy, her refreshing splash,
moistening flesh.

A-a-ah! The lee of land; calms the tempest and relaxes my strength, a cooling breeze,
trembling knees.
Tired and wet; I gratefully stand on her opposing shore, demanding friend,
the journey's end.

Streaking down the boardwalk; her sweet smell fills my memory, Her glistening beach,
within reach.

A security fence; blocks my path to heaven's gate, heart wrenching grief, no relief.
Outstretched hands; Her voice calls with requiem song, upon yearning ears,
desirous tears.

The following poem was written for Mrs. Marsha Kujawa, who held a district position in the Ohio Order of Eastern Star. The names in Italics were the names of different groups within the district. The following was written for future reading of a fond memory.

MY TREASURE CHEST OF DREAMS

I tripped up to my cerebral attic, and opened the squeaky door.
Then tip-toed across old wooden planks, and dust bunnies on the floor.
A beam of light poked through a vent to a corner nest,
And shed a little glimmer; a glow, on an old hope chest.

I popped its golden hasp, and two latches on the sides,
And opened the heavy cedar lid to dreams which tried to hide.
The flying dust shot like *Shooting Stars* in the illumination.
Or was it magic fairy dust in a vivid imagination.

I gazed into the cedar chest as its fragrance filled my face;
And saw *Gingham Dogs* chase *Calico Cats* at a frenzied pace.
Behind the cats and dogs ran *Officers of Animal Control*.
To capture all with nets, and save their wondering souls.

I saw *Cheery Cherubs* taking aim with their arrows and bows,
At angels with outstretched wings and slightly tarnished halos.
The light in the vent has started to dwindle on the dizzying din,
Taking away the pleasure of the friends that I found within.

It's time to close the treasure chest of dreams, for I know I'll find,
All those precious memories locked in the attic of my mind.
And those fond memories I'll come and visit every now and then,
When shaking firm hands and getting warm hugs from all of you
My Friends.

The following six poems were written while waiting for the opening of an Ohio Eastern Star Meeting of which I was an Officer. Each poem was of something that had happened recently or about the season. Each one was recited at the same meeting.

OLD AGE !?!?

He can drive a truck, get your drawers unstuck,
And assist you in raking the leaves.
He'll work for hours replanting your flowers.
His favorite channel is Public TV.

He can do a 5 K run, and play ball in the sun,
And when he's thirsty he'll drink your tea.
He's really bright and will stay up all night.
Its hard to believe he's going on three.

SPRING THINGS

I've seen the twinkle in my bride's eyes
I've seen the colors of the Aurora shoot by.
I've heard the growing pains of my granddaughter's cry.
I know of the Master and the way He died.
I've felt the power in the touch of a friend.
And the smiles on their faces that their kindness extends.
Though I've seen, and heard, and felt, I still need to beg
From anyone who can show me a rabbit lay an egg.

BALD

If we have less do we have more?
You can probably say that if we snore.
But—can you say that if you shave your head?
I 'spoze you could if you think instead,
That it gives all the Lassies, Ms, and Misses,
A special place to put their kisses.

God Bless Green

Green is more than Irishmen.
Green is a jealous lover.
Green is precious emeralds.
That looks stupid on old rover.
Green is for our economy.
Green is for the clover.
Green is what we dream about,
'Cause winter is almost over.

PIECES OF AUTUMN

Splashes of color fill the lanes.
It dazzles the eyes and amazes the brains
The air changes to brisk and cold.
It chills the spine and challenges the bold.
Harvest time makes fruit markets full.
Pies of pumpkin and apple make me drool.
Time for the shuffle of little feet.
Rushing our doorsteps yelling "Trick or Treat".
. . . Thank God !

WHO'S THE LITTLE BEGGARS?

It wasn't that long ago when I went tripping through the leaves,
Running up to houses yelling "Trick or Treat".
Now I walk my Grandkids around the block and back,
To hear them yell for goodies, and later, I raid their sack.

THE BIKE RIDE

I love the thunder in the bike I ride
Soft hands 'n legs on my sides.
A scold in my ear when I rub her thigh
Then she squeezes me; wonder why?!

You cannot imagine . . . how high.

Down twisting paths 'mid the trees,
Sometimes peppered by flies and bees,
Enjoying the smells sure to please,
While cruising within the forest breeze.

You cannot imagine . . . how high.

The deer running back in the bush.
The opposing cars passing, "Swoosh!"
Up the hill, "Engine, give a push!",
I'm glad the road is smooth and flush.

You cannot imagine . . . how high.

The non-biker just doesn't know
Why this love can heal your soul.
How the power and the purr.
For many an illness I have a cure.

How high? . . . *NIRVANA*

A Slow Ride

I took a slow ride today,
For they went miles for me.
Slow down; show respect;
For they paid so you live free.

They wrote a blank check
And then raised their hand
Giving everything they own
To preserve this great land.

Forfeiting their house, their car,
Maybe their husband or wife;
Everything they hold dear,
Including their own life.

So, take the slow ride today
Behind the Patriot Guard bikes,
Behind all the Firefighters,
And the Police with flashing lights.

Or, stand quietly on the curb
And wave your flag high.
Say a little prayer for them
And salute as they pass by.

Heroes are far and few between
For the price they have to pay.
Show respect for the fallen heroes
And take a slow ride today.

AU REVOIR

by Marie E. Sneider

Goodbye, Summer.
I loved your smiling sun
And your heat, too,
And the white clouds floating
In a sea of blue.
I can't forget the stilly night
And the distant stars
Gleaming, cool, and white.
I loved you then,
As I shall again
When you come, heralded by April's rain.

TO AN OLD MAN

By Marie E. Mackley

Sitting there,
In your rocking chair
What kind of dreams
Are you having?

Are you planning the future
Or living the past?
Or just enjoying
The task completed?

ROLLING THUNDER— MEMORIAL DAY WEEKEND—2011

The following is my first trip to Washington DC and Rolling Thunder. A patriot biker rally to encourage more search and recovery of the MIAs / POWs. I have a dilemma. It's not about writing an article; it about writing about every feeling that can touch a person to the soul. Hmmmm, Bold Words!

JOY!

Packing the bags and loading the bike onto the back of my old, rusting 98' Ford Ranger in anticipation of an interesting 5 days in Washington DC. Rain was the forecast so the Custom will just have to sleep till another day. A hundred questions pop through my hairless head. How many bikers are going to be there? Do they all ride Harleys? Will my 94 Honda V45 Magna fit in? Wonder what the monuments and attractions are all about? Will the pictures on TV and in books be like the real thing?

Accompanying us (Susan and I) was Dan Nolan, the Junior Past Director of Hudson Falls American Legion Riders (ALR) Post 574, and his wonderful wife, Dee. Dan was selected, with a couple others earlier in the year, to lay a wreath at the Tomb of the Unknown Soldier for all the members of the ALR. Talk about Joy and Excitement. I've only seen that on television by Our President and other Heads of State. What an honor! Its 10am, hot and muggy, but off we go streaking down the Northway in my non-air conditioned truck. The traveling was smooth with only a couple stops for the usual, until we arrived in one of the several interstate loops that surround DC. I believe it was the Holiday weekend escape by the area residents as traffic crawled, bumper-to-bumper for miles. We finally arrived at the Resident's Inn about 7pm after 2 hours sitting in hot, slow-moving local traffic. WOW! Sure looked forward to a cold beverage, relaxation, and a soft chair and bed.

ANTICIPATION

It's Friday morning and we're organizing a plan of attack on the Capital. First, Breakfast at the Silver Diner, where we can discuss logistics. The plan is to ride the bikes into DC and find a spot to park. "No Problem!" I am told by the 'regulars'. "We just ride into the Mall area and park in the grass just off the road." Dan said. "A-a-a-ah, Okay!! And that's alright with the local Security?" I said. "You'll see." I was told.

Three things you need going into Washington DC; sunscreen, water, and sneakers. We are going to do lots of walking and boots would be crazy. It was hot and humid Memorial Day weekend, but we didn't seem to mind as we were wide-eyed and eager to race into DC to see the sites.

AWESOME

As we roll over the Roosevelt Memorial Bridge and onto Consti-
tutional Avenue I am at awe by the enormity of the area and the
sizes of the Memorials. Just across from the Lincoln Memorial we
park our bikes in a well shaded, grassy area on the corner of Henry
Baker Drive and Constitutional Ave. with about 100 bikes. That is
interesting! I'm NOT the only one with a rice-burner! Aaahhh, I
feel better now.

Off we go and if we become split-up, we know our way back. First
agenda is the Lincoln Memorial. There, I re-learned that Lincoln's
main objective wasn't freeing the slaves, but maintaining the Union
of all the states. To keep together this democratic form of government,
the republic that was unique to the world, and fought so in creditably
hard to maintain by earlier generations. It was Lincoln's Emancipation

Proclamation made our Constitution stronger and freed the slaves. I soon would be reminded of the many, many generations to follow who would also fight hard.

I cannot place all the pictures needed to impress on you this and other National Treasures. Every American should witness this collection of our Country's endeavor for FREEDOM that is displayed in the Washington DC's National Mall Area.

> GOD WILLS THAT IT CONTINUE UNTIL ALL
> THE WEALTH PILED BY THE BONDSMAN'S
> TWO HUNDRED AND FIFTY YEARS OF UN-
> REQUITED TOIL SHALL BE SUNK AND
> UNTIL EVERY DROP OF BLOOD DRAWN WITH
> THE LASH SHALL BE PAID BY ANOTHER
> DRAWN WITH THE SWORD AS WAS SAID THREE
> THOUSAND YEARS AGO SO STILL IT MUST
> BE SAID "THE JUDGMENTS OF THE LORD
> ARE TRUE AND RIGHTEOUS ALTOGETHER."
> WITH MALICE TOWARD NONE WITH CHARITY
> FOR ALL WITH FIRMNESS IN THE RIGHT AS
> GOD GIVES US TO SEE THE RIGHT LET US
> STRIVE ON TO FINISH THE WORK WE ARE IN
> TO BIND UP THE NATION'S WOUNDS TO CARE
> FOR HIM WHO SHALL HAVE BORNE THE BAT-
> TLE AND FOR HIS WIDOW AND HIS ORPHAN-
> TO DO ALL WHICH MAY ACHIEVE AND CHER-
> ISH A JUST AND LASTING PEACE AMONG
> OURSELVES AND WITH ALL NATIONS·

The last paragraph rather sums it up starting, "With malice towards none . . .". Today, is it any different?

GRIEF

I cannot express how this next place is etched in my memory. It's the "Thankless" War; the Vietnam War Memorial. I had three classmate's names on that wall; just three out of a graduating class of over 600. Three friends I hung out with, played ball together, and even dated the same girl; that girl later became my wife. Now, it is not casual memories; it's personal.

Just a dark, shining black granite wall with over 58,000 names of someone's friend, someone's husband / wife, someone's father / mother. Half buried granite lined end-to-end with roses for Memorial Day remembrance. I couldn't stay there very long and walked head-bowed, tears streaming, over to the familiar Vietnam Soldier's statue; a tribute to our fighting men in the military at that time.

A pause, a reflection, a hallow feeling as we follow the sidewalk to a newer memorial that does not have the recognition it deserves; the Vietnam Nurse's Memorial.

Oh, those Angels in fatigues, who suffered not just the sounds of war, but sheltered and ministered each and every wounded or dying soldier they encountered. While standing there a little lady about my age walked up to me. She said, "The hat that is worn by the girl kneeing down . . . there in the back.

That hat was worn by only the MASH nurses at the start of the Vietnam conflict, and became a standard for the troops in the field. I know," she said. "I was a nurse over there, then." I gave her a big hug and thanked her before she walked quietly on her way.

Oh, the crossroads of the people we meet and the little things that mean so much. I wonder if she will ever be over the pain of combat I felt in our short chat.

With feet sore, knee hurting, mouth full of cotton balls from thirst, and tear ducts flushed almost dry we needed to head back to the hotel.

EXCITEMENT

Saturday, on this day we planned to visit Arlington Cemetery, and witness Dan place a wreath on the Tomb of the Unknown Soldier. We travel in Rte 50 across the Roosevelt Bridge, around the Lincoln Memorial, across the Arlington Bridge where we noticed hundreds of bikes and many more people. Since the Tomb and everything else is uphill from the entrance, we decided to take one of the many guided buses available. After six months of anticipation we were all excited for Dan who bought the wreath, transported it safely there, and was just about running to the site to lay the wreath at 11am.

This is an extremely solemn site. To show respect for the fallen, there is no talking, no chewing of gum, and you are encouraged not to make any commotion.

The guard is changed with precision on a regular interval. The guard's uniform is checked, the rifle is closely inspected in a strictly regimented routine. Being very meticulous would be an understatement. Note the brown stains in the marble walkway from the precise path taken each pass. Even during the last hurricane that swept the Washington DC area, the guards refused to leave their post.

At the laying of the ALR wreath by Dan, the wreath was presented by the Head Guard marched to the center of the Tomb area, where Dan and others met the Head Guard for hanging and playing "Taps" by a lone bugler. Shivers ran through me and I tried to be still enough to take the pictures.

Afterwards we waited for the shuttle and more explanations of the Cemetery's history. On Memorial weekend, an American flag is placed by each and every one of the over one million graves in Arlington's 1100 acres. America has paid a monumental price for Freedom. Embrace it!

FUN TIMES

Arlington took most of the day. Since the day was hot and tomorrow would be the parade we needed to go back to the Hotel and prepare for the evening party. American Legion Riders of Post 574 puts on a little hot dog and burger feed for those at the hotel. None other than Dan Nolan is the head chef. Let the party begin! All residents of the hotel and ALR from Ohio, Kentucky, Pennsylvania, and many other States attend. Attendees claim that they enjoy the commradry so much they return every year to that hotel for the fun Post 574 puts on. Nice compliments, fun, food, laughter, and refreshment lasted into the late hours. Sorry, no pictures as we were having too much fun.

EMPOWERMENT

Sunday, Parade Day, the day when bikers gather from all over the country to "Ride to the Wall" and encourage the release of our POWs and return of our MIAs throughout the worlds battle grounds. The parade starts at noon, but the preliminary set-up starts at 8am in the parking lots of the Pentagon. Some decided not to ride in the parade due to the heat and the 9 – 10 hour day. The roads are blocked off by the DC Police for nothing but the bikers and emergency vehicles. Dignitaries from all walks of life join in the parade.

I would show you more pictures of the parade, but they would look similar to this.

At noon, streams of bikers riding at about 25 mph on all kinds of motorcycles cross the bridge and ride down Constitution Avenue, to Pennsylvania Blvd, to Third street (which runs in front of the Capital Building), and back down (and away from the Capital) Independence Ave. There is a growl, a thunder, heard no matter where you are in the National Mall area and echoing down the side streets of Washington DC. Pedestrians while site-seeing scurry to cross the roads in between groups of bikers. A steady stream of bikes thunder around the Mall area, and none go around a second time. Three hours after its start I happened to stop and talk to a Lady Police Officer. She said the police keep in communication with the Pentagon parking lots and that the north (and last) parking lot had just started to empty. At 3:45pm a few police cars follow the end of the parade signaling they all had finished. Those who monitor the parking lot estimated there was a quarter of a million bikes in the parade this year. The news media estimated there was a half million bikers in the area that year.

We walked the Mall area one more time, and took a few more pictures of the WWII Memorial. How open and friendly it looked. Visitors soak their tired feet in the cool fountain's waters.

No names of soldiers, just statements of prominent people in the war. Families brought displays of cardboard sheets on which were pictures of relation who fought in the war and leaned them against the perimeter. A collage of foreign encampments with groups of soldiers that probably friends of the individual. Families that wanted to share with the world their loved one(s).

A huge bronze rope tied together all the columns representing the states and possessions that took part in the war.

Although I had close friends and relation that were in WWII, I didn't feel the loss which I felt at the Vietnam Wall. I'm sure those who lived through WWII felt like I did living through Vietnam.

EMPTINESS

I need to finish with this point, so I saved an interesting part till last. We visited the Korean War Memorial also. How spooky this appeared. Granite walls line one side of the walkway, with sculpted soldiers in ra-ingear walking out of a wooded area on the other. Troops trudging up a hill to . . . somewhere. Spooky gray figures carrying weapons, some with radios, and some with med packs.

Ghostly figures that reflect off the granite wall. Is this a warning of the future?

A granite wall with hundreds of faces etched randomly within. This is a worry-some, chilling art-form. If you stop and think, since WWII, we have not had a decisive victory in any war or conflict. We have not conquered anyone, or anything, or actually want to. We have only tried to support Freedom for others from the oppression of bad regimes.

This brings me the final granite slab placed at the end of the Korean Memorial.

Take heed all of America.

To maintain Freedom it may take some from each generation. The Common American has sacrificed so much over the 235 + years of this Great Union. More financially and with their blood than any corporation, government, or formal institution can ever repay.

Therefore, what price will we have to pay? What does the future hold for generations to come?

Pray for our children.

Thanks for your time.

Prose vs. Poetry

Poetry *nou.* **Wikipedia definition**

1. the art of rhythmical composition, written or spoken, for exciting pleasure by beautiful, imaginative, or elevated thoughts.
2. literary work in metrical form; verse.

Poetry is language spoken or written according to some pattern of recurrence that emphasizes relationships between words on the basis of sound as well as meaning. This pattern is almost always a rhythm or metre (regular pattern of sound units). This pattern may be supplemented by ornamentation such as rhyme or alliteration or both.

Prose *noun* **Wikipedia definition**

1. the ordinary form of spoken or written language, without metrical structure, as distinguished from poetry or verse.
2. matter-of-fact, commonplace, or dull expression, quality, discourse, etc.

Prose is the form of written language that is not organized according to formal patterns of verse. It may have some sort of rhythm and some devices of repetition and balance, but these are not governed by regularly sustained formal arrangement. The significant unit is the sentence, not the line. Hence it is represented without line breaks in writing.

I feel the definition of poetry today seems to be lost. Most so called poetry today does not require the need to rhyme, or have meter. Thus it can be very close to normal writing. Please read the following example of normal writing.

Autumn Motorcycle Riding in the Adirondacks

The air is cool and thick with moisture as I ride in the mountains of the Adirondacks. It seems to make this ride much more meaningful. The beautiful colors of the leaves and the fragrance of cedar, pine, and aspen fill my senses. Yet, I know it will not last long, as in a few weeks the leaves will be down and the trees bare. But today, I am going to enjoy the long ride through the twisting mountain roads. The sound of the motorcycle seems to be deeper, mellower, and much more soothing. It's a very pleasant sound that soon will be silenced by the upcoming winter.

The following is to help you distinguish between the Poetry and Prose, and in some cases this task can be very difficult. I have left rhyme and meter, key aspects of good to great poetry, out of the examples so it is more apparent as to the differences. So I ask you, is the following Prose or Poetry?

Autumn Motorcycle Riding in the Adirondacks

The air is cool and thick with moisture,
As I ride in the mountains of the Adirondacks.
It seems to make this ride much more meaningful.
The beautiful colors of the leaves,
And the fragrance of cedar, pine, and aspen fill my senses.
Yet, I know it will not last long,
As in a few weeks the leaves will be down,
And the trees bare.
But today,
I am going to enjoy the long ride,
Through the twisting mountain roads.
The sound of the motorcycle seem to be deeper,
Mellower, and much more soothing.
It's a very pleasant sound,
That soon will be silenced,
By the upcoming winter.

The first and second paragraphs are Prose, "straight forward meaning". It is normal writing with complete sentences containing colorful words. The second paragraph is a cut up version with more commas and breaks, still in sentence form, and the wording is identical; therefore it is also Prose.

The following piece carries the same information, with much less words, and what would seem to be incomplete or fragmented sentences. This is poetry even though it does not rhyme or have any meter. It leaves the reader with mental pictures which the writer injects and allows you to 'fill in' its meaning. Everyone's understanding can be different or, " . . . in lieu of, it's apparent meaning."

RIDING AUTUMN

Oh heavy autumn air,
How you make my ride that much sweeter.
Passing your majestic fragrant foliage;
Dazzling the eyes of this witness.
Your stay is short; my yearning long.

Far I ride, twisting, turning,
Color-splashed mountain roads,
And ponder the deepened music of the iron horse.
Stay music,
Stay awhile,
As I fear the upcoming snows.

I prefer poetry that has rhyme and meter, and requires much more time to create than the above (which I wrote in about 15 minutes). Rhyming poetry is song the orchestra enhances. Poetry is happy, sad, prophetic, and witty. Poetry can make you laugh, bring you to tears, and encourage you to ponder aspects of the author's thoughts; be they passionate, hateful, or whimsical.

"When you write in prose, you cook the rice. When you write poetry, you turn rice into rice wine. Cooked rice doesn't change its shape, but rice wine changes both in quality and shape. Cooked rice makes one full so one can live out one's life span ... wine, on the other hand, makes one drunk, makes the sad happy, and the happy sad. Its effect is sublimely beyond explanation."—Wu Qiao

GLOSSARY OF BIKER TERMS

American Iron: An American made motorcycle.

Bags: Saddle Bags

Bandana: A handy piece of cloth for many different uses. To cover the head to absorb sweat like a Dew Rag, to cover the face against the elements, to keep the cold or rain from one's neck area, handkerchief, bandage, or any handy use.

Brain Bucket or just **Bucket:** A helmet.

Cager: Driver confined in a car or truck.

Colors: The main patch on the back of a jacket or vest displaying the group a rider belongs to, or rides with.

Crotch Rocket: Sport racing bikes usually 1000cc or less and produces high whining RPMs.

Dew Rag: a bandana or type of cloth to cover the head to absorb sweat.

Fart Sack: Sleeping bag.

Fat Man Straps: the chain(s) that hold the front of a vest or jacket together. Allows good flow of air on hot days.

Fishheads and Rice: Asian Motorcycles.

Flyin': Riding fast down a road.

Grease Groove: The center of the road lane that collects the grease and oil from vehicles that is not worn off by their tires. Bad place to ride as oil can build up on Motorcycle tires and makes it difficult to stop.

Highway Pegs: Foot rests that allow the rider to stretch out on a highway for comfort.

Iron Horse: a Motorcycle.

Ol' Lady Pad: The seat behind the driver. Also known as 'The Throne" or "Maxi Pad".

One Percenters: Its believed one percent of bikers are outlaws or habitual law breakers.

Riding Bitch: The act of riding as a passenger on a motorcycle.

Riding Lanes: On the right or left side of a road lane usually clean of oils and trash.

Road Cruiser: A bike that is used for long distance riding. Usually has a CB radio, Luggage box and saddle bags, GPS,
Stereo radio / CD player. Also known as a '2-wheeled RV'.

Road Rash: Skin sliding on a road surface leaving a rash.

Rubber Alligator: Re-treads that have peeled off some vehicle and left on the road.

Rubber: The tires.

Rugged Old School: A bike assembled with the bare minimum to ride on the road. No shocks, side panels, sometimes no rear fender, no windshield, few if any gauges.

Saddle: The driver's seat on a motorcycle.

Scoot: Short for Scooter. Another name for a motorcycle.

Sissy Bar: The back rest for the passenger is more to keep them from falling off.

Skins: Leather clothes.

Suicide Shift: A gear shift lever in which you have to take your hand off the handlebars to shift.

Tar Snake: Tar poured in a line to fill cracks in a road surface.

Trike: a 3-wheeled bike with 2 in the front **or** rear of the bike.

Twisting the Wick: Turning the right handgrip to accelerate.